David Sears

Contrabands and Vagrants

David Sears

Contrabands and Vagrants

ISBN/EAN: 9783743347908

Manufactured in Europe, USA, Canada, Australia, Japa

Cover: Foto ©ninafisch / pixelio.de

Manufactured and distributed by brebook publishing software
(www.brebook.com)

David Sears

Contrabands and Vagrants

CONTRABANDS AND VAGRANTS.

DEAR SIR,

We have never, heretofore, exchanged letters; not, I am sure, from any want of mutual good feeling, but simply because no special reason made a correspondence necessary.

At the present moment, the case is different; and it is the duty of every citizen, however situated, to contribute his mite, however small, to assist his country in her day of trouble.

The result of the present conflict can

hardly be doubtful, notwithstanding our present reverses: but when the Federal troops shall hereafter have full and quiet possession of the Border States, and the power of secession is thus far wiped out, the struggle is not over; the end is not yet.

I take it for granted, that, in the Free States, the baneful effects of slavery on our institutions, habits, and morals, are now so evident, that the people, grown wise by experience, will with unanimity vote to repeal that portion of the second section of the first article of the Constitution which relates to representatives and taxation; and, under the leading vote of Congress, will limit the power to hold persons to service or labor, in any of the States, to the present living generation of slaves.

The Constitution, being so amended, will make its provisions more in accordance with the spirit of the age, and the moral convictions of twenty millions of people. And certainly the people have *now* a right so to amend it, to suit themselves; the seceded States having voluntarily thrown off their allegiance, and declared that they will not live under the Constitution as it is, will not amend it or reconstruct it, and are in open rebellion to get rid of it.

But the most vicious of these States, now commonly called the Gulf States, are the least capable of self-government, and have few of the necessary ingredients to make a nationality. *Separated from the United States, they are nothing,* and, in all essential matters, must be subject to it; nor is it at all improbable, that, after the lapse of a few years, they will finally pray to be re-admitted to the Union, even with the amendments above named, which may at the time be a part of its Constitution.

Is it not, then, wisest for the United States, when she has brought the Border States under control, to cease from further hostilities on land, and consolidate her rule by the Congressional action above named, and satisfy the Border States by the enactment of a law for the gradual emancipation of slaves, based on the plan suggested in the letters to the Hon. John Quincy Adams, and herewith enclosed?

The proposal may be offered after the liquidation of the cost and charges of the war, and *as a compensation* to those States in which the laws and Constitution of the United States are the ruling government; but open also, on the same terms, to the remaining outlying States on petition, and acceptance of the amended Constitution.

The following synopsis of the plan for emancipation, proposed by me, many years ago, to the Hon. John Quincy Adams, then a member of Congress, gives a sufficiently clear view of the process of action to serve as a foundation to commence on under existing circumstances. It was prepared by some writer in New York, on his own responsibility, and, I believe, had a considerable circulation. It received my acquiescence and approval.

But, before proceeding to suggest any amendments of the Constitution, the proper move is to carry out the action proposed by Major-General Butler, in his late communication to the Secretary of War, dated a few days since, relative to " contrabands of war," and slaves fleeing to us for protection.

The general order subjoined, properly drafted, might be immediately issued from the War Department to the several military commands in the service of the United States, and arrangements made for

suitable depots in selected parts of the Free
States, preparatory to the issue of billets
by their several executives.

General Order. — When fugitive slaves
come within your lines, or when slaves are
seized by your men, as contrabands of war,
while working for the rebel forces, they
are to be marched to the nearest depot
provided for the purpose, and thence, under proper regulations, distributed among
the Free States, in the ratio of their population; to be billeted by authority of the
State executives upon the inhabitants, freeholders, as domestic laborers, as follows:
viz., males between ten and twenty years
of age, and females between six and twenty-
five years of age, to freeholders in the cities.
These household laborers, of whom not
more than two are to be billeted on any one
family, are to be employed in light labor, as

cooks and chambermaids, and in other in-
door-work; and are to be returned to the
order of the United States at the end of the
war, if not previously disposed of among
the freeholders, in accordance with their
several hopes and wishes.

Persons of a more mature age may be
billeted on the farmers in the Free States,
and especially on those of Pennsylvania,
Ohio, Indiana, and Illinois, as farm-laborers;
and elsewhere on request of freeholders.

If some such measure is carried out by
the Administration at the proper time and
in proper places, the strength and spirit of
the rebels will be paralyzed, their counsels
divided, and our arms triumphant. It af-
fords, also, a practicable stimulus to a final
adjustment of our difficulties: for the experience of every day renders it more mani-
fest, that the Gulf States cannot be brought

back willing and faithful members of the Union; and they must, therefore, be reduced in every way, and their means of offence crippled, until necessity produces a sounder judgment, and conviction follows administrative weakness.

The Cabinet, so supported and encouraged by the people, will go forward with double power; and, while by the above course the rebel is properly chastised, the loyal citizen, under the emancipation plan, will be honored and rewarded.

The following is the plan for a gradual emancipation, before alluded to, published in New York, 1857. It may be of use as a form of compensation to be applied to the Union men of the South.

GRADUAL EMANCIPATION;

PUBLISHED IN NEW YORK, 1857.

THERE has been so much said and published on the subject of Emancipation, both at the North and South, that it has become somewhat difficult to discuss it without awaking party interests and feelings. The best cause, as is well known, may be ruined by injudicious advocates. The people of the South, however, cannot but approve of candor and truth; and we feel confident that they will be pleased with the Hon. DAVID SEARS's safe and liberal propositions on the subject of gradual emancipation, advocating, as they most clearly do, not only a full indemnity for every slave liberated, but presenting no impossibility or serious difficulty of execution.

Some of the extracts from the letters of Mr. Sears seem almost prophetic.

Before presenting our readers with the substance of Mr. Sears's plan for emancipation, we insert the following petition in its support, which, we understand, is now in circulation for signatures in this and several other of the States: —

"*To the Senate, and House of Representatives, of the United States of America.*

"The petition of the undersigned, citizens of ——, respectfully asks, that you will consider the expediency of endeavoring to effect such a change in the Constitution or Laws as shall appropriate the public lands of the nation in aid of the extinction of slavery throughout the Union.

"Also the expediency of appointing commissioners, whose duty it shall be — under such conditions as Congress may determine — to purchase and emancipate slaves, being female children born prior to ——. And also of making annual appropriations by law for the purpose, on a pledge of said public lands, with a declaratory act, that from and after —— there shall be no hereditary slavery; but that, on and after that date, every child born within the United States of America, their jurisdiction and territories, shall be born free."

In one of Mr. Sears's late communications on the subject of emancipation, when giving statistical facts in relation to it, he says,—

" The last census of the United States gave 420,000 as the number of female slaves under ten years of age, and 390,000 as the number of female slaves between the ages of ten and twenty years. The

plan proposed contemplates the purchase
of one or both of these classes, at a price
to be agreed on. It is estimated, that, at
their present average value, they could be
bought and emancipated at a cost much
less than the expense of the last war of the
nation with Great Britain, and for less than
the probable cost of the late Mexican War."

A summary of the plan is as follows : —

1. *Congress to appropriate the proceeds
of the sales of public lands to the extinction
of slavery.*

2. Commissioners to be appointed by
Congress to negotiate with the Legislatures of the Slave States for the purchase
of female slaves under ten years of age,
and also, if necessary, female slaves under
twenty years of age ; and *with instructions
to close a contract with any one of said States*
which may agree to accept the terms of

their commission. *The money to be paid to the States*, and to be by them apportioned.

3. Female slaves so purchased are to be free, and their issue are to be free.

4. In consideration of the above, all children born after —— are to be free, within the States so contracting; and, from that date, *hereditary slavery in the United States*, its territories and dependencies, *is to cease*.

5. In order to avoid the difficulties and dangers which might arise from an immediate and unqualified liberation of a debased and ignorant class, I have suggested that children who may be born after —— should be apprenticed to their owners or others until they are twenty-one years of age, on the proviso that they receive from their masters a suitable education to fit them for their improved condition. And this is to apply to all children born after that period, whether their mothers

have been freed by appropriations made
by Congress or not.

The spirit of Mr. Sears's plan of emancipation is contained in the above summary.
In our own judgment, we have arrived at a
conjuncture in which the wisdom of our
greatest statesmen is required on this
subject.   The present scheme transfers
the burden from the slaveholder to the
nation.   Thousands at the North will be
found to aid in the accomplishment of a
peaceful emancipation, even to the extreme
of self-denial and sacrifice.   Mr. Sears's
plan has not been prepared under the
influence of any sectional or party feeling.
The warmest advocates of the present
state of things must be satisfied of this,
after reading his excellent and judicious
letters on the subject; as they show most
conclusively, that the evil can be gradually

abolished without detriment to their rights
or interests. We invite the attention of the
press and our public men to the consideration of the plan proposed. May nothing
cloud the prospect of the nation's coming
to a speedy, united, and happy decision!

A late number of the "Norfolk (Va.)
Herald" contains the following remarks of
its candid and truth-speaking editor: —

"Let those who are lured by the prospect
of gain, or who really believe that they
can better their condition by emigrating to
the new States, follow their bent, and take
their slaves along with them! The vacuum
may cause a momentary weakness; but it
will be only to recruit with twofold vigor.
The place of every slave will, in time, be
filled with hardy, industrious, tax-paying,
musket-bearing freemen, of the right stuff
to people a free State, — *which Virginia
is destined to be, one of these days; and*

the sooner (consistently with reason), the better for her own good."

This is cheering intelligence from such a quarter. The people of Western Virginia, whose prolific mountains and valleys encourage the growth of the spirit of freedom, have long wished to be rid of slavery; but the people of Southern Virginia, more unfortunate in location and association, have hitherto successfully repressed this Western sentiment. If, as would appear from this paragraph from the " Norfolk Herald," the true character of slavery, as a ruinous absorbent, is beginning to be felt, there is indeed hope of Virginia.

That it would be " better for her " if slavery were abolished in Virginia, there can be no reasonable doubt. Slavery is, and always has been, an incubus upon the prosperity of that State. Her originally rich soil has become barren and fruitless under the exhausting and improvident tillage of slave labor: the once prolific plantations are bankrupting their proprietors. To thousands the unpleasant alternative is presented, of abject poverty at home, or emigration to the new soil at the West. Large numbers have chosen the latter, and their places have been filled by farmers from the North. They, schooled in the science of agriculture and inured to toil, can with free labor restore what slavery has exhausted. Under their judicious application of this free labor, Virginia would soon be lifted from her present condition; and, when this truth shall be felt and acted upon, the "Herald's" prediction will become matter of history.

With these and a multitude of similar facts before them, will not the intelligent and reflecting people of the slaveholding States take into serious and candid consideration the plan devised and recommended by Mr. Sears for the removal of the originating and operative causes, which, as long as they continue to exist, cannot, according to the apprehensions of the wisest men who have lived in the Southern States, fail of being deeply injurious to their present prosperity and happiness, and of being instrumental in placing invincible impediments in the way of their future advancement in science, literature, the arts, in wealth, and in every thing else which can justly be deemed promotive of an increased degree of safety, comfort, civilization, and refinement?

We more cheerfully make these reflections, from the well-known fact that such illustrious men as Rufus King, while United-States senator, and more recently the distinguished Henry Clay, have boldly and honestly expressed similar sentiments.

The terms proposed are liberal. Mr. Sears remarks, "We would manage it, if possible, so as to gain the approbation of the most interested, and be prepared to meet them on terms of mutual concession for common preservation. COMPENSATION MUST BE MADE FOR EVERY EMANCIPATED SLAVE, and an obnoxious feature in the Constitution removed." Now, if our Southern friends would meet the demands of this proposal fairly, manfully, in due season, and in as kind a spirit as animates the author of the plan alluded to, the one great trust devolving on the men of the present generation in this country would be accomplished; and, in ages to come, their posterity would bless them.

In order to present more clearly the views and sentiments of Mr. Sears in relation to his proposed plan for emancipation, we give the following extracts from his correspondence on the subject with the late Ex-President, John Quincy Adams : —

"We believe that the interest as well as happiness of the whole Union requires the abolition of slavery. But in this belief we would be careful to let neither prejudice nor passion nor wrong govern us. We desire, therefore, that some proposal may be made, to show to the intelligent and thinking part of the South, that, in the adjustment of this matter, the rights of property are to be sacredly respected; some mode · adopted to satisfy them that our intentions are honest; some evidence given that we act under a conscientious conviction, that on it depends the quiet and duration of the Union."

"To avoid the inevitable result of an open outbreak, it is necessary that there should be a united action in the Free States, with the adoption of some great principle which shall unite us all."

"In this view the enclosed principles are framed. They are independent of party, and leave every one free to act on all minor questions; being united only in this, *that, from and after ——, every child born in the United States shall be born free.* This great object we earnestly seek to obtain in a reasonable way, and upon principles of right and justice. We would manage it, if possible, so as to gain the approbation of those most interested, and be prepared to meet them on terms of mutual concession for common preservation. Compensation must be made for every emancipated slave, and an obnoxious feature in the Constitution removed. But it is not necessary, in attempting this, to touch the argument, that a certain interpretation of that instrument would perpetuate slavery to all generations unborn; nor to show, that, by such an assumption of construction, *the State of Virginia* and her Southern neighbors—while the traffic is expressly forbidden elsewhere—are virtually made *another Africa* for the supply of slaves, and have a monopoly of the trade. Such irritating topics may be put at rest. It is best to appeal to the interest of the slaveholder to convince him. It is proposed that he should be paid for every slave that is emancipated; and that he shall have the labor, *during their lives,* of such as are not purchased. He is, in fact, deprived of nothing which has existence, or in which he can have property. No pecuniary sacrifice is exacted; the expense of the infancy of children being paid by indenture with their mothers, who, being purchased and made free, may bind them to labor, as we bind our apprentices and an honorable opportunity is thus offered to the slaveholder to test the honesty of *his* democratic principles, and *his* regard for human rights, without danger and without loss. The moral tone of the slave is raised by the brighter future, and parent slaves are induced to behave well, and to work hard, in the knowledge that their children will be free; all tending to the benefit of the owner."

" No proposition like the present has ever yet been made to the South, nor remuneration in any shape offered. Let us try it, in the spirit of conciliation, to save them and ourselves from a great, a common, and an impending calamity."

" These views I have strongly urged; and I have endeavored to impress on the minds of our friends the necessity of uniting on the subject of compensation, for the sake of union, happiness, and peace."

" It certainly appears to be a matter of great importance, especially to the three States (Maryland, Virginia, and Kentucky), to look closely into the subject, and examine the proposition tendered to them. They are Border States, and in contact with a spirit of freedom ; and, while they are becoming comparatively less rich and strong, they cannot but see that their neighbors, divided from them only by an imaginary line or a small stream, are rapidly advancing upon them in wealth and strength. Nor can they deny that these consequences follow, on the one hand, from the institution of slavery; and, on the other, from the institution of free labor.*   The

* What a volume is contained in the following contrast! and yet this is only a fair statement of the difference between a Slave and a Free State : —

former must ever yield to the latter in the production of wealth, prosperity, and

FREE SOIL. — MASSACHUSETTS.

Has Territory	7,500 sq. m.
Population in 1845	800,000
Products in do.	$124,735,264
Production to each Individual	$154
Cost of State Government, 1844	$461,097
Members of Congress	10
Scholars in Common Schools	160,257
In Academies	16,746
In Colleges	769
Persons over twenty who cannot read or write	4,448
Slaves	NONE.

SLAVE SOIL. — SOUTH CAROLINA.

Has Territory	25,000 sq. m.
Population in 1845	600,000
Products in do.	$53,086,765
Production to each Individual	$88
Cost of State Government, 1844	$347,831
Members of Congress	7
Scholars in Common Schools	12,520
In Academies	4,326
In Colleges	168
Whites over twenty who cannot read or write	20,615
Slaves not permitted to read or write	330,000

Still more striking does this contrast become if we compare Kentucky and Ohio, — sister States alike in soil and climate, and divided only by a river, but as dissimilar in enterprise and prosperity as can be imagined. No powers of argument can reason down facts like these; and already is their influence at work in Virginia, Kentucky, Maryland, and perhaps other States. Conciliation, as well as firmness, is now demanded on the part of the North, — firmness in an opposition to the extension of slavery, but a generous and conciliatory spirit in devising a method of relief for the States now involved in it.

power.   As these elements of greatness
increase among the free States, what, in all
probability, will be the future destiny of
these Border States?"

"I wish not to excite an angry feeling,
or to wound the self-love of any one; *my
object is peace:* but if the people of these
States would calmly hear what may be said,
and coolly judge of what they hear, we
should all, in time, come to the same conclusion.   Suppose this conclusion arrived
at: then Maryland, Virginia, and Kentucky
would unite in applying to Congress for
the very compromise which the petition
offers.   They would say, 'We have long
borne the burden of slavery, and now wish
to get rid of it.   We cannot do so without
your assistance.   We may, it is true, sell a
part of our property in South Carolina and
other States, where the soil, from its nature,
and the climate, from its unhealthiness,

can only be inhabited by the African; but we have been at a great expense in rearing the infant to the child, and in feeding the old man in his age. You must, therefore, grant us something as an equivalent; and we will meet in the spirit of compromise, to root from our land an acknowledged evil. Put us, we pray you, in a position to reap the full advantages offered to us by Heaven in a healthy climate and a rich soil, and to this end purchase and make free the female infants of our slaves, and we will *abolish hereditary slavery for ever.* Every child born after —— shall be born free.'"

"Nor is the supposition of such a union of opinion by any means chimerical. It is obviously for the interest of these three States to range themselves on the side of freedom; and, if they should do so, the result is certain."

"As events ripen, it is evident that no

time should be lost in devising some conciliatory measure of compromise.   The
great question of slavery, though in a mo-
dified form, has already been brought before Congress, never again to quit it until
slavery ceases.   The power and number of
those who seek its extinction are daily on
the increase, and the chances of compensation for slaves will yearly grow less:
after ——, in my opinion, none can be ob-
tained.   The matter must then assume a
more serious aspect, and the Border States
will doubly suffer."

"In a letter to a friend,* who, in a series
of numbers recently published in the 'Boston Courier,' has so fully demonstrated the
value of the plan of emancipation I suggested, and who has touched the subject

* Henry Lee, Esq , of Brookline, formerly candidate of
South Carolina for the Vice - Presidency of the United
States.

with a master's hand, I frankly stated my fears; and, in giving them also to you, I trust they will be received as they were uttered, — 'more in sorrow than in anger.'"

"It seems to me that we are slowly but steadily advancing to that dreadful crisis which has been so long predicted. The events of the next ten years will probably decide the question of the continuance of South Carolina and some other of the Slave States as a part of the confederacy; for, by that time, the North will demonstrate a determined force against slave dictation. The balance of power under the compromise of the Constitution is gone; the Constitution itself is invaded and broken; and new elements are introduced into it, which are too inflammable in their nature not to consume it."

"The right of slave representation, originally limited in fact, if not by name, to five out of thirteen States, is soon to be extended over conquered territories and foreign nations of more than half a continent. The indolent and ignorant slaveman, without education or industry, is hereafter, by means of a three-fifth vote, to guide the destinies of this mighty empire."

"Had a firm resistance been shown to the admission of Texas, while demanding a *slave representation* (I do not say a *slave population*, — that is another branch of the question, — but a slave representation), there is little doubt that the war with Mexico would have been avoided. What is now to prevent a slave representation from being indefinitely extended? what to prevent the farmer and mechanic of the North from being ruled and governed by the slaves of the South? Nothing but a stern and unbending will, followed out by action, to maintain the principles of the Constitution. Mutual concession and compromise may do much; but can they be brought to bear, except under pressure of necessity, and to save the Union?"

"Events are tending to this issue, and sooner or later the struggle will come. It is impossible that three-fourths of the talent, the wealth, and the industry of the country can always quietly submit to have their petitions and counsels rejected, and their best interests and their own peculiar institutions continually sacrificed at the will and pleasure of the feudal bondage-power of slavemen. We had better meet the evil, however great, or in whatever form it may approach us."

"I do not fear a dissolution of the Union. The worst that can happen is a temporary secession, from the confederation, of certain of the Slave States, which may perhaps quit us for a time, and attempt to form an independent government. Let them try the experiment. In five years from their separation, they would be completely at our mercy, and petition for re-annexation on our own terms. They cannot exist without us; yet being with us, and of little comparative value in the statistics of power and the elements of greatness, they govern us at their own caprice."

" We are, in fact, in a false position. We have yielded up the compromise of five Slave States to eight Free States, — the spirit of the compact of the Constitution, — and permitted a gross encroachment of the slavemen upon the degree of power we originally conceded. But notwithstanding these facts, and the feelings they naturally engender, I am anxious still to offer to them the plan for emancipation which you have been kind enough publicly to notice. It was conceived in good-will and friendship to the South, and offered in the spirit of mutual concession, to avert an impending evil, and restore harmony to the Union."

"No one understands better than yourself, whose experience extends beyond the era of the Constitution, that the present state of hostility between the North and South has mainly been brought about by a British policy, and the radical sentiments uttered by the feudal chiefs of South Carolina and other Slave States, and thrown by them as firebrands among us, to light the flames of riot, and spread abroad the embers of disunion. They have been successful, and we have retreated before them."

"Their huzzas for liberty to all, and equality for each, have been taken by us literally; and we hasten to shout them back in earnest. Men north of Washington cannot comprehend why the doctrine should not

3

be good south of it; and what the slaveman has preached, the freeman is now determined to practise."

" Had the educated and intelligent of the South, instead of rushing to their ruin in a vain struggle for personal power, been willing to have remained friends with the same class of the North, and jointly labored with them in the construction and maintenance of a government of laws founded upon reasonable and liberal principles, and unitedly opposed the intrigues and management of vicious and needy men, who have nothing to lose and every thing to gain, how much more happy would have been our country, and how many bitter feelings would have been spared to her best and bravest!

Quem Deus vult perdere, prius dementat."

The annexed article, from the editor of the "New-York Chronicle" of Aug. 15, 1857, may be perused with profit: —

We gave an account, in a late number, of the movement to free the country of slavery by paying to the masters the price of their slaves out of the proceeds of the public lands. The feasibility of such a scheme, in the midst of so many passions and conflicting interests, we regard as extremely doubtful. It certainly cannot be consummated without an amount of agitation of which it is impossible at present to conceive. It is well, however, that it is in the hearts of any to attempt it; and we wish well to the meeting which is to convene at Cleveland, O., to discuss the subject.

It is, perhaps, a favorable omen that this scheme is by no means a new one. It was broached some years ago by Hon. David

Sears, of Boston. Mr. Sears addressed a
letter at the time to John Quincy Adams;
issued documents on the subject from the
press; and considerable attention was excited to it by these means.

The plan was summarily this: "To purchase and emancipate slaves, being female
children born prior to 1850; and to make
annual appropriations by law for the purpose, on a pledge of the public lands, with
a declaratory act, that, from and after 1850,
there shall be no hereditary slavery, but
that, on and after that date, every child
born within the United States of America,
their jurisdiction and territories, shall be
free." Mr. Sears estimated the number of
female slaves to be purchased, under ten
years of age, at 420,000; and between the
ages of ten and twenty, at 390,000: one or
both of which might be purchased. As
their children would be born in freedom, it

would require but a generation or two to insure the extinction of slavery from the country. This purchase would be made with less cost than our last war with England, or for less than that of our war with Mexico.

Mr. Sears would intrust the carrying-out of the plan to commissioners especially appointed for the purpose, who should be empowered to appropriate the proceeds of the public lands to the object, to negotiate with the legislatures of the Slave States for the purchase of the female slaves, and to close a contract with any one of said States which might agree to accept the terms of their commission; the money to be paid to the States, and to be by them appropriated. The slaves so purchased, and their offspring, should be free; and the children born after a certain date should be declared free.

Mr. Sears's plan is based on this radical

idea of acknowledging a *pro-tempore* right to property in slaves, but denies the right to hold a *race* in bondage through all future time. To avoid the evil of unqualified liberty in the hands of an ignorant, debased people, he would have the children of these emancipated females apprenticed to their owners or others till they were twenty-one years of age, on the promise that they receive from their masters a suitable education to fit them for their improved condition.

As we said before, we fear that the passions enlisted forbid the hope of a calm, impartial consideration of any plan whatever. Excited men and terrified horses are alike : they dash ahead, till their course ends in ruin and revolution. They will not stop calmly to estimate the tendencies of things, and to provide a safety-valve for the escape of the element

which is driving them to destruction.
Party, prejudice, and passion apart, and
what wisdom, what safety, what justice,
would all see in some such plan as this! It
would make all parts of the country mutual
burden-bearers in disposing of an evil which
all have been, directly or indirectly, con-
cerned in introducing. It would indemnify
those who have been encouraged by our
laws to invest their property in slaves
against loss. It would secure society at
the South against the dreaded evils of in-
stantaneous emancipation, and give both
the dominant and the servile race time to
adjust themselves to this new condition of
domestic freedom. It would immediately
open the floodgates of the South to the in-
flux of free laborers to cultivate their rich
soil; to work their mines; to occupy their
waterfalls with machinery, villages, and population; to construct railroads on a scale

commensurate with what they are at the North; and to enable them to vie with us in the glorious competition for pre-eminence in subduing the land which God has given us, and extending to all the races of men that boon of liberty which is the pride and the boast of our country.

Nothing but the prospect of indefinite bondage south of Mason and Dixon's line, and the consequent disrepute in which labor is held, restrains the emigrant masses from Europe and the Eastern States from making that their home, that the theatre for expending their capital, and that the seat of their enterprise, thrift, and population. But for this single cause, Kentucky might be as populous as Ohio, Virginia as Pennsylvania, and Norfolk might vie with New York in commerce and opulence. The Transatlantic Ferry about to be established at the South, would, in that case, enjoy the patronage of those crossing the ocean, now so exclusively extended to Northern lines of steamers.

The law of compensation for slaves liberated may be based, according to circumstances and with proper accountability, on the following general principles; viz. : —

Bonds of the United States, of $500 and upwards, are to be issued, on which interest at six per cent is to be allowed until the original sum is doubled; from and after which, and on presentation and cancellation of the original bond, a new certificate shall be issued in accordance with the sum cancelled.

These second bonds are to be paid off as follows ; viz. : —

At the end of the first six months, three per cent of interest and one per cent of capital is to be paid, to make up the sum of four per cent on the bond; and, at the end of each succeeding six months, three per cent of interest on the unpaid capital, and a sufficient sum from the remaining capital, is to be paid, to make up another sum of four per cent on the bond: and this process is to be continued until the whole sum, principal and interest, is paid.

The above stock pays eight per cent per annum to the holder until the whole debt is liquidated, and is similar to the old six per cent deferred debt of the United States.

In the hope that the suggestions here made may not be entirely without use in your discussions on this difficult subject, I have the honor to remain your humble servant,

DAVID SEARS.

Hon. HENRY WILSON,
    Senate of the United States.

www.ingramcontent.com/pod-product-compliance
Lightning Source LLC
Chambersburg PA
CBHW032137080426
42733CB00008B/1108